Directory of Paying Markets
for
Freelance Writers

2018 Edition
by
Julie G Marie Scott

About the Author

Julie Scott is a retired tax preparer and a prolific freelance writer. A former teacher, she holds a Bachelor's Degree in education from Worcester State University and a Master's Degree in communications from Boston University.

Mrs. Scott lives in Central MA, USA, with her husband. They have two grown sons. Julie is the author of several eBooks. She is available via email at write2earn@aol.com or at her website: www.write2earn.net.

Table of Contents

<u>Legalese</u>

Information in this directory is true and correct as of the day of the entry. However, since the internet changes on a dime, it is important to keep this in mind as you follow the information and live links in this directory. There is no intention -- stated, implied or otherwise -- to deceive or mislead anyone accepting this work as it is for educational and informational assistance only.

Education, Information and Income

Thorough investigation went into this presentation to give freelance readers and writers the best chances to connect with target markets for their career-building opportunities. When I began researching and writing, the task became one of vetting each entry.

You must remember one vital item as you embark on your journey -- guide in hand. The goal of the report is educational as well as informational and the author claims no responsibility for loss or damage occurring as the result of using this information. If, by using this directory, you experience an adverse outcome, please consult with a specialist in the area of your concern.

Finally, if you should find contradictory information within these pages, please document the inconsistencies. Submit your findings to the site owner as well as the author of this directory. Should you have any questions or concerns, please contact the author at:

write2earn@aol.com

Your corrections will undergo new research before any changes appear in future updates. When you pay for your first issue of the directory, future updates come to you free of charge. If you wish to be on the update list, send your name, proof of purchase and BEST email address to me:

write2earn@aol.com

The information herein points out that there is work for writers in a variety of arenas. Some may not be obvious at first sight. Writers looking for income should apply to the paying markets that enthuse and energize their inner muse.

Content writing markets are changing rapidly mostly to keep up with new Google algorithms. Most of these markets may return later. For now, they are working on transitional moves and are not in this version of the directory. Please realize that income sources change as fast (or faster) than the world turns.

All rights to compilation, analysis, distribution and income from the directory remain the property of this author/compiler. Many research hours went into the inspection of each site in order to bring timesaving information to writers most in need of assignments and income.

Therefore, please respect the work done on your behalf and refrain from copying, packaging, offering as a bonus, selling, editing, claiming, changing or creating new products from this report without the express permission of the author.

<u>Directory of Paying Markets for Freelance Writers</u>

Many styles and types of freelance writing exist. A short list of niches in freelance writing is below. Some chapters in this directory will have directions or commentary as you delve further into the information available.

Mathematically, the shortest path between two points is a straight line. Users should focus on the straight line going from the input of effort to the outcome of earnings. An asterisk (*) indicates a market with very lean competition as well as decent earning capacity.

Diligent research will help you uncover an area of special appeal where you could possibly establish yourself as an expert. A passionate writer with dedication to career and personal success would be able to earn a reasonable income as a freelance writer within a niche specialty. Some of specialty niches include:

Academic writing - Article writing - Blog writing

Business writing - Copywriting - eBook writing

Editorial writing - Essay writing - Financial writing

Grant writing - Ghostwriting - Letter writing

Report writing - Review writing - SEO writing

Sports writing - Technical writing - Tutorial writing

Tip/List writing - Travel writing - Web content writing

White paper writing

About This Directory

This directory is for the freelancer seeking writing income without time to research those sources. A writer should be writing rather than attempting to FIND writing, which is an exercise in the fine art of wasting valuable time. The goal is to uncover and present sites that pay article writers, content writers and bloggers to do what they do best ... write.

The lists of sites within the directory are within the niches on the previous page. This directory began with a dozen sites scribbled on a post-it-note - until I found some search terms leading to places where researchers could find the rest of these sites. I saw several chapters emerging upon turning over many promising rocks.

The result includes definitions with examples of existing sites where writers are welcome to apply. As more sites come online, an update will make it into your hands IF those sites meet certain criteria for inclusion.

The inclusion of any site is contingent upon meeting certain subjective, albeit reasonable, criteria. These include elements such as being writer-friendly, clearly displaying writer guidelines that are easy to follow and noting deadlines that are reasonably scheduled. They must also show the compensation for each type of assignment. If you know of a website that meets this inclusive criteria, please contact the author at write2earn@aol.com.

Code within the Treasure

I personally use many of the sites listed in this directory. My current favorites change from month to month. Each day when I make my rounds, my favorites are the sites where I concentrate my efforts. If you also wish to sell some articles for a price you pre-determine, pay special attention to the brackets.

Databases leading to many writing sites are on the last page of the directory due mainly to the fact that it is impossible for one person to inspect every one of the listings. However, on the advice of other writers, I did include some entries that they found loosely fit my criteria as set out in the section above.

Live Links to Websites

Live links within this directory will lead you to content company websites that offer a flat fee for written material in most cases. You will not find listings of bid-for-work, residual income or passive income sites. This does not mean you should never use them. However, it does mean you should look at other resources to find dependable work if you are writing for passive income. Above all, time spent bidding for work does not produce any income.

So, whether you write articles, short blog posts or product reviews, remember that you are writing *for payment*. In a more practical light, you need that money to live. Writing is not only fulfilling, but is also the path to earning what you require to survive and thrive.

NOTES: Investigate entries of interest, understand the expectations of each site and perform your own diligent inspection before you consent to write any content they might request.

Sites that require full and complete "sample" articles as part of the application process should be at least partially suspect.

Avoid potential piracy of your work by running your articles through CopyscapePremium.com (publish them to your website or blog) as insurance that no one can use your samples illegally.

A few sites that request complete articles in order to apply for writing work appear in this chapter. However, the samples they ask from each applicant are short and *off-topic*. Still, it is very important to pay attention to your gut feeling because not all sites are fit for every writer.

If you locate a listing in the directory that explains their guidelines, compensation or terms different from the information at a destination website, please follow instructions on the legalese page and notify me:

write2earn@aol.com

I will address the issue quickly and appropriately.

Some titles have a presence both online and offline - magazines or newspapers - AND with specific writer guidelines appearing online. They publish some articles online and others in a hard copy edition. Be aware that in most cases, they only pay for one format.

Directory Listings

Long-time professional and traditional print writers give a bad rap to content site/content mill writers. That should not stop anyone from writing for one or more of these listings:

2camels.com is a travel publication that is open to writers worldwide. It has both an online and hard copy version of each issue they put to bed. Compensation is $20 per 500 words. http://www.2camels.com/writers-guidelines.php

AListApart.com seeks writers worldwide for high quality articles and pay $200 for articles that meet their quality level for publication. http://alistapart.com/about/contribute

AuctionBytes.com is the site for writers worldwide who can write short descriptions of 100-500 words with a call to action. Compensation is $20 per article. http://www.ecommercebytes.com/cab/pages/write/

BackToCollege.com is a site especially for adult learners returning to college for a degree or advanced studies. They pay $65 for all unsolicited articles. http://back2college.com/guide.htm

BiblioBuffet.com is for writers worldwide who have a penchant for reading and love to write about it in 600-6000 words. They offer $10-$25 per written work. http://about-bb/write-for-us-mainmenu-255

BleacherReport.com seeks sports writers from the United States only to write articles for their site. Pay ranges per quality. http://bleacherreport.com/writer_application

Blue Mountain Arts is a site that publishes well-written poetry by writers worldwide. They compensate poets at $50-$350 per poem. http://www.sps.com/help/writers_guidelines.html

Cashwriter.net accepts writers worldwide for articles of various lengths. Pay is contingent on amount indicated and acceptance or rejection of your article. They pay in the double digits and negotiate reasonable payment with the writer. http://www.cashwriter.net/register/?type=writer

CellPhoneForums.net is for writers worldwide who know everything there is to know about cellphones, smartphones and similar devices. They compensate their writers with $75 per review according to their guidelines.
http://incomebooster.org/cellphoneforumsnet/

Ceramics.org is the website of the American Ceramic Society looking for United States writers to submit articles of 1,000 to 5,000 words for compensation of $350 to $950. http://ceramics.org/publications-and-resources/the-bulletin/write-for-the-bulletin

Chicken Soup for the Soul does not limit the location of their writers and offers compensation of $200 per passionate story for their website or hard copy format. http://www.chickensoup.com/story-submissions/story-guidelines

Clickworker.com is a site for writers worldwide who are available for short writing tasks and equally low pay. (It is included here to fill in the gaps when you wish you had something to write.)
http://www.clickworker.com/en/clickworker?customer=falso

CoffeeBreakforWriters.com is a site for writers worldwide who write for other writers. It offers payment of $15 for a 500-word article.
http://coffeebreakforwriters.com/writers-guidelines.html

Conjecture.com welcomes writers worldwide who are willing to research and write 400-word articles for $10-$14 per article.
http://www.conjecture.com/about.htm

Copify.com works with writers from the United States and the United Kingdom. Although the pay is initially low, the longer an article remains unwritten, the higher the payment rises. A writer may not know when an article initially becomes available because notifications go out (in email form) after the article goes unclaimed for a day or two. http://us.copify/copywriters

Cracked.com accepts writers worldwide who can produce articles in the style and tone of this publication. If you write an article and it makes the front page, the author receives very decent compensation.
http://www.cracked.com/write-for-cracked/

DailyCrowdsource.com does not say their writers are country-specific, but their subject matter seems to have a United States focus.
http://dailycrowdsource.com/content/crowdsourcing/1208-you-are-the-hero-crowdsourcing-needs

DeveloperTutorials.com accepts writers worldwide and pays $30-$100 per article or tutorial. http://www.developertutorials.com/pay-per-tut.php

DollarStretcher.com works with United States writers on topics guiding the reader to get more for their money. Compensation is $0.10 per word. http://www.stretcher.com/menu/writers.cfm

DotWriter.com seeks writers worldwide for blog posts and articles on many and varied topics for content as buyer or seller. Three writer levels are available with compensation unique to each level. This is perfect for beginning/student writers. http://dotwriter.com/

DropZone.com seeks United States skydivers who will write 1000 words for $30-$100 an article. http://www.dropzone.com/about/Dropzone.com_Article_Submission_Guidelines_694.html

FabJobs.com works with writers from the United States and Canada who are able to write career guide eBooks for them. Compensation is $1500-$2000 per career guide. http://fabjob.com/writers.html

FreelanceWriting.com is very non-committal about writer locations. However, they compensate writers at $25 per article upon acceptance of an article. http://www.freelancewriting.com/write-for-freelance-writing-dot-com.php

GardeningKnowHow.com looks for gardeners worldwide with real experience. They hire from March to May only, but accept applications and emails all year long. They pay well and make a commitment at the time of inquiry by a potential writer. http://www.gardeningknowhow.com/garden-writer/

GoodOleBoat.com welcomes boaters worldwide who speak English as a 1st language and can write 300-5000 word articles for their various departments. Payment ranges from $50-$700 per article per department. http://www.goodoleboat.com/writers_guidelines/

GreatContent.co.uk with headquarters in Germany, accepts writers who are able to write in British English. (greatcontent.de, greatcontent.fr, greatcontent.co.uk, great content.it, grearcontent.nl, greatcontent.es, **greatcontent.com**, greatcontent.com.br). Payment varies with assignment and is available through PayPal after the writer's account reaches £25. https://www.greatcontent.co.uk/guidelines

GreenPrints.com is a quirky site for small gardeners and welcomes writers from Canada and the United States. Compensation is a maximum of $150 per article they accept for online or offline use.
http://www.greenprints.com/content/12-writer-guidelines

Guideposts.org appears to accept writers worldwide who receive $100-$500 per narrative for online or offline use. http://www.guideposts.org/writers-guidelines

HireWriters.com hires writers worldwide with English as the native language. They compensate for 150-300 words at $5 per article.
http://hirewriters.com/signup/writer

IndianLife.org looks for Native North American Indian writers for a range of topics, styles and tones. Depending upon your choice of department, articles will vary in length from 100-2000 words with payments ranging from $30-$150 per article. They accept fillers.
http://www.indianlife.org/index.php?option=com_content&task=view&id=121&Itemid=32

iWorkWell.com welcomes United States writers for articles that pay upwards of $200 as well as a bio that links to articles that you write.
http://new.iworkwell.com/smes/

LookingForClues accepts writers worldwide for articles of 800-1600 words and pays those writers $10-$20 per article.
http://www.bkserv.net/LFC/WriteForLFC.aspx

LoveToKnow.com accepts writers worldwide who can write 600-word articles for compensation of $20 per article. http://www.lovetoknow.com/write-for-us.htm

MakeMoneyinLife.com is a relatively new site that accepts articles of 400 words or more and compensates the author with $32 per article. There is no mention of author location, but this appears to be an international site.
http://www.makemoneyinlife.com/write-for-us

MatadorNetwork.com accepts worldwide writers for travel articles with a compensation of $0.50 per word. http://www.matadornetwork.com
MediaShower.com will accept writers whose native language is English and who are willing to write 500-900 words for $25 per article.
http://www.mediashower.com/Content?Action=WriterApp

OnlineWritingJobs.com looks for writers from Canada and the United States who can write articles in a variety of areas. They offer compensation ranging from $15-$50 per article. Payment must be mutually agreeable before you accept the assignment. (Formerly QualityGal.com) https://www.onlinewritingjobs.com/why-write-for-us/

Scripted.com gives no specific location for writers, but does expect quality delivered on time every time. Compensation is $20-$35 per article. http://scripted.com/our-writers/

SitePoint.com looks for worldwide writers with articles over 1,500 words. They accept articles about web development from high-quality freelance writers for a flat rate of $100 with a possible click-through bonus of $250. http://www.sitepoint.com/write-for-us/

Skyword.com gives no specific location for their writers, but quality writing is an expectation. They pay $35-$50 per article and share revenue with the writers. Initial application should be to their Gather News department. http://www.skyword.com/create-for-skyword/

StrategyPage.com accepts writers worldwide to write about conflict/war strategy in 200-1000 words. Compensation is $20 per item submitted ($0.02 to $0.10 per word). It is important to examine their site because repeat information is unacceptable. http://www.strategypage.com

SurvivalLife.com is not specific about writer location. However, they have both an online and offline presence. Compensation is $25 upon acceptance. Be careful of the editors because they have no idea how important the fine art of communication is for their writers. http://www.survivallife.com

Textbroker.com will accept writers from various countries of origin. They start everyone at level three for compensation of $0.01 per word per article. There are five levels, but level five is for professional writers requiring almost no edits. http://www.textbroker.com

Textmaster.com is a fairly new site with better pay than most. It appears that writers worldwide can work here. Pay range is from 3.9 cents to 15 cents and higher. http://www.textmaster.com

ThemeForest.net welcomes writers worldwide for both their online and offline publication. They seek quality English language articles and offer compensation ranging from $100-$150 per article. http://themeforest.net/make_money/become_an_author

TransitionsAbroad.com welcomes writers worldwide who provide well-written cultural immersion articles that are individualized and are not sightseeing travel articles. Articles are for both online and offline publication and pay $50-$150 upon acceptance.
http://www.transitionsabroad.com/information/writers/writers.shtml

TravelGeneration.com welcomes writers from New Zealand only. Well-written travel articles earn $50 upon acceptance.
http://travelgeneration.com/footer/get-paid-to-travel/

TutToaster.com accepts submissions only from United States writers. They pay $10-$25 per article upon acceptance. NOTE: There is no guarantee of acceptance. http://www.tuttoaster.com/write-for-us-and-get-paid/

UX Booth.com is a site for both new and seasoned United States authors who can produce 1200-1800 words per article according to guidelines. They have an online and offline presence with payment of $100 for publication in either place. http://www.uxbooth.com/contribute/

VentanaMonthly.com accepts United States writers only for both their online and offline publications. Articles accepted for publication are 400-1500 words in either place and writers receive $0.20 per word.
http://www.ventanamonthly.com/writers.php

VisitSouth.com is a site for United States writers who live in any of the Southern states and wish to contribute a post with an image. Compensation is $15 per post. http://www.visitsouth.com/locals-application

Vivilia.com accepts writers worldwide for articles of at least 400 words each. They have a pay range from $3-$20 per article.
http://www.vivilia.com/en/node/freelancers

Web-content-provider.com encourages participation by writers worldwide who speak and write English as a first language. More information can be yours with an inquiry through the website. http://www.web-content-provider.com/web-content-writing.php

Windowbox.com seeks writers from Canada, United Kingdom and the United States to write short articles of 200-400 words each. Compensation is $10 per article. http://www.windowbox.com/resources-links/blogs-publications

WordGigs.com accepts United States writers who speak and write English as a first language. Compensation is $4 for each 400-word article. http://www.wordgigs.com/

WordsOfWorth.org seeks writers from Australia, Canada, United Kingdom and the United States to complete various briefs for their clients. Compensation is unique to each project proposal. http://www.wordsofworth.org/apply-to-be-a-writer

WorkOnlineBlog.com pays $50-75 for articles that contain tips for those who are working online or from home. https://workonlineblog.com/get-paid-to-write/

WorldStart.com accepts United States writers with a forte in technology. Payment is $25-$50 per tech tip. http://www.worldstart.com/writers-guidelines/

Write.com seeks United States writers to fulfill client requests. Responding writers will receive the payment schedule. http://www.write.com/

WriteFromHome.com accepts United States writers for both online and offline publication. Compensation is $25 per article upon acceptance. It is a database of writing sites, which accepts information writers. http://writefromhome.com/

WriterAccess.com seeks United States writers to complete client requests. The pay is unique to each assignment. http://www.writeraccess.com/writers-about/
WriterMag.com accepts submissions from United States writers only. Articles can range from 300-3000 words each. Compensation stretches from $25-$500 per article depending on the department or column. Writer resources, articles and prompts are available on the website. http://www.writemag.com/the-magazine/submission-guidelines/

WritersDomain.net accepts writers from Canada, France, the United States and Australia to complete articles for their clients. Compensation for articles of 200-250 words is $20. http://blog.writersdomain.net/writing-guidelines/

WritingForDollars.com accepts writers worldwide to complete articles of 500-1000 words. Compensation per article ranges from $15-$25. http://www.writingfordollars.com/GuidelinesDB.cfm

Writing-World.com seeks writers worldwide to complete 800-2000 word articles. Compensation is $0.075 per word, which caps at $150. Humor articles pay $20. http://www.writing-world.com/admin1/guidelines.shtml

Note to Readers:

As I noted at the beginning of this directory, there are some major changes here. Some sites no longer appear in this edition of the directory and new ones are taking their place. The internet is a rapidly changing virtual world and an awareness of the fluidity is important.

The sites that are no longer here have succumbed to one (or all) of the following:

The compensation dropped to the point where it is hardly worth the time and effort to write for them.

They are not currently working with new writers.

The site no longer exists

Compensation shifted from flat fee to passive income

Applications exceed available positions for freelancers

For those reasons, I had to pull some entries from this section. However, if you know of a site that should appear here, please contact me:

write2earn@aol.com

Academic Writing

This is likely the most controversial writing that a freelancer might consent to do. Although the payment is a cut above other forms of writing, the moral issues compromise ethics that affect most writers. Each freelancer needs to balance the need to earn money against the student choice to "buy" a diploma or degree.

Two important angles apply to academic writing: argument and analysis. Those angles always begin with a statement or claim that will prove itself through logical argument and/or methodical analysis. Solid information, depth of research and attention to deadlines are a strict requirement of this type of writing.

Moral, Ethical or Shady Practices

If you wish to pursue academic writing, you can do so without compromising your ethics or morals. No stigma exists that would stop a writer from producing material for the classroom teacher. Writing for the sole purpose of guiding classroom success gives a "feel good" aura to this writing.

Sometimes this writing could entail lesson planning for teachers or assistance with the development of units that include props for classroom use.

Another source of academic writing comes from textbook publishers who often contract with writers to obtain research, fact-checking and information they intend to publish for classroom use. It is legitimate academic writing with the offer of decent compensation. Inclusion of this type of writing in the directory is not an educational, ethical or moral statement.

Making Sense of It All

Today, many parents make the choice to home school their children. They are grateful for any information or props available to them. The pursuit of some academic writing does make sense for writers: transcribing, formatting, editing and proofing work that is fundamentally complete.

Remember, parents are the first teachers a child encounters. Anything you can do to enhance this experience for parent or child is a worthy endeavor.

Parents are highly teachable and creative people, but most are not professional educators. They need and want guidance as well as lesson suggestions. These homemade teachers often use a blueprint design that advises or explains the concepts within a unit of study, but that does not mean that they understand those concepts.

Selective writers with an open mind can easily choose topics for this audience. Professional teachers or curriculum specialists gravitate toward this market and are a perfect fit as writers. However, you do not need that background to help in the process of education.

Ethical Issues

In the past, educated academic writers dealt with essays, reports, term papers, thesis, college applications, scholarship essays and dissertations. Today, the market is flooding with student requests for writers to do classroom work for them. (No one did undergraduate or graduate writing for me.)

When I finished my studies, both the degree and the accompanying bills were entirely mine. This is the way learning happens … by design. Professors are smart people and can easily recognize work that the student did not do.

A respectable writer will not participate in this conspiracy to commit fraud under an academic shield. Strong morals, ethics and the strength of conviction will help you avoid this type of writing.

You Have Options

Dinosaurs laid the trail that textbooks are following. Modern units of study are in the form of articles, syllabi, lesson blueprints, workbooks and suggestions for completion. Techniques can apply to economic tourism as well as academia.

Textbook publishers, home schooling parents, classroom educators, travel agents and tour group operators can all find benefits in the new format presentations.

Three potential situations for writers include:

Bookbuilders of Boston accept United States writers with curriculum knowledge or teaching experience. Payment is project-specific and agreed in advance. https://www.bbboston.org/

Education.com accepts writers from the United States who will write 600-800 word articles. Compensation is project-specific and negotiated in advance. http://www.education.com/about/jobs/

CatholicTeacher.com welcomes writers in the United States who will write 600-1500 words to earn $100-$250 per article. Various departments are available to writers. You can download the writer guidelines in PDF format to see guidelines for each department.
http://www.catholicteacher.com/contacttodayscatholicteacher.html

Most freelance writing projects focus on elementary level education (ages 5-12) and junior high or middle school (ages 12-14). The listings here are only a few sources available to freelance writers. Visit, evaluate and do your research before submitting a query and an application.

As you can see, a freelance writer can choose many different directions if you have a desire to pursue the field of academic writing. For those who "think outside the box," creative ingenuity will open up some fulfilling pathways within the field of freelance academic writing.

Blog writing caught the pen of professional writers a few years ago (2006-2009). Then, sometime during 2013, blogs began to populate the writing real estate in cyberspace. Businesses began using them to inform customers or potential clients about industry-specific topics.

The new mantra is that a business without a blog is a business about to close. Customers today spend more time shopping on the internet for goods and services than they ever did before this. Blogs may have beginnings as journal rants, but they have evolved into some authoritative and informative communication devices.

Writers who saw the vision as a trend toward online journal entries emerge and grow are now making a decent income as professional bloggers. Business enterprises use blogs to inform users about products and services that are available - or about to become available - to the customer. Emerging technology will define the blog, determine what it will be and its overall use.

Blog Writers and Guest Posters

Small business owners generally do not have the time or the skills to keep a blog current. However, they will hire a blog writer or blog content provider to do this for them. Most business websites now have the word "blog" on the navigation bar.

The weblog is a short journal entry consisting of 100+ words with a link to the full article on a page within the website. These entries are available through the maintenance effort of individual writers or teams of writers (collaborative blogs) with a common interest in a niche topic. Collaborative blogs invite professional guest posters to submit articles for a certain team blog.

Open-System Blogs

Open system blogs are much like forums and require moderation. Most of these positions require an obvious presence to keep posts on-topic. Moderators find it helpful to have a few rules for posters to follow, which are reminders to "play nice" with no fighting over a difference of opinion.

Generally, the blog contains a homepage with the most recent posts and an archive of older entries. Topical blogs are quite popular and focus on a narrow niche of topics with loyal followers.

Thousands of blogs now occupy the internet covering topics as diverse as college life, space exploration, politics, conflict/war, science, technology, books and information, coins, currency and precious metals.

Buzz About Blogs

Weblogs are not new. They have been around since the late 1990s. However, new software and hosting platforms come together and create an easier posting experience. This led to the explosion of weblogs from 2000 forward.

Except for blogs geared to journalists, these articles are offering significant niche information for a specific user. At times, posts might discuss news found elsewhere and link to the original article. This causes the weblog to resemble an editorial in a newspaper rather than a traditional news article.

Journalism … or Not So Much

Some blogs seem to be amateur journalism, but most are merely commentaries or editorials. An effort is out there to use newspaper articles as links "of distinction" by connecting to the original article written by a journalist. This could actually enhance a post and that is not a bad thing.

Linking lends credence to the opinion of the poster and the point of view that the article contains. By linking to newspaper articles, readers from countries around the world, who would not normally have the time to read them, can gain some perspective on the reporting of well-written pieces. Readers with an interest in a topic can go to posts and archives for current and historical news.

Whether you perceive weblogs as journalistic pursuits or not, media companies feel the impact of them and an awareness of their value is rising.

Blog Posting vs. Article Writing

Blog posts are short and informative, rarely exceeding 400 words. An article is usually much longer, formal and requires research, writing, editing, proofing, praying and payment. The blog has the experience of a warm and winding journey to the position it occupies today.

Finally, some sites pay guest bloggers real money. This started as a challenge from one freelance writer who felt that blogging professionals are real writers and she dared blog owners to treat them as professionals. Since then, certain blog sites began to pay these professional blog writers. Certain sites are now paying $50 or more for a guest post from a professional writer.

Blogs That Pay Real Money

Be a Freelance Blogger seeks guest posts for this blog with the same expectations - high quality writing. Compensation is $50 per guest post on an appropriate topic. http://beafreelanceblogger.com/guest-blogging-guidelines/

BlogHer seeks bloggers worldwide to submit a post to one of the topics listed on the guidelines at this site. They pay $50 and will license and syndicate your post. http://www.blogher.com/marketplace/opportunities/syndication

Blogmutt.com is a community of writers from the United States, which provides blog posts to clients and incentives for writers who accumulate points to move from one level to the next. Compensation is $8 per post. http://www.blogmutt.com/pages/writer

Foxyblogger.com accepts writers worldwide to participate in their program. http://foxyblogger.com/dashboard//active-jobs/

Ghostbloggers.net seeks US-based, native English speaking ghostwriters to write for compensation of $3.50 per 100 words (300 words equals $10.50). http://www.ghostbloggers.net/?page=sell

HorseChannel.com is a website for horse industry care, essays or news and more. Compensation is $25 to $100 per article. https://workonlineblog.com/get-paid-to-write

iWriter.com has a wide selection of titles for writers worldwide - and each posting pays $15. http://www.iwriter.com/signup.php?wrt

MakeaLivingWriting.com welcomes bloggers worldwide who have English as a first language. A contribution must fit the topic of the blog site. Payment is $50 for 500 words. http://www.makealivingwriting.com/why-i-pay-writers/

MoneyPantry.com is a blog about earning, saving or growing your money in some unusual ways. They seem to accept writers who can be paid $30 to $150 via PayPal.com. http://moneypantry.com/contribute

Mountain Blog is for the mountain gear community and recreational mountain activities they are/have been experiencing. The articles that Mountain Blog accepts for publication receive $50 in payment. http://www.mountaingear.com/themountainblog/meet-our-bloggers/submission-guidelines

OnText.com accepts bloggers worldwide who can write posts in grammatically correct English and are a good fit for client requests. Compensation is $50 per guest post. http://ontext.com/writerguidelines/

ReadLearnWrite.com accepts writers worldwide as guest posters to write about writing for $50 per blog posts. https://readlearnwrite.submittable.com/

SHTFBlog is a survival information blog that pays $50 to North American writers. "We are currently seeking survivalist, craftsmen, firearms enthusiasts, outdoorsmen and all around skilled people to become contributors for SHTFBlog & Survival Cache." http://www.shtfblog.com/write-for-shtfblog

Snapt.net seeks tutorial content (complete with images and screenshots) from writers worldwide who follow the guidelines for compensation of $50 each. Articles should match their products at the website. http://kb.snapt.net/get-paid/
SnowsBest is a blog for people who live in the snow belts around the world. The compensation for some articles is $50. http://www.snowsbest.com/contribute

Strong Whispers is a multi-topic blog site that expects high quality, well-written posts by established English-fluent freelancers using grammatically correct English. Compensation ranges up to $50 per post. http://strongwhispers.com/get-paid-to-write-articles/

TakeLessons is a blog that connects teachers and students. They invite writers to their team of teachers to write 500-800 words for compensation of $50 per article. http://takelessons.com/blog/submission-guidelines

Work Online Blog is for writers who submit articles in grammatically correct English. Each article pays $50 for 1500 (or more) words.
https://workonlineblog.com/get-paid-to-write

YourOnline.biz wants bloggers worldwide who have English as their first, native language. They are looking for well-written articles that are a good fit for the topic of their blog. Compensation is $100 per guest post.
http://youronline.biz/guest-posts-wanted-100/

Catch Me If You Can

Bloggers, who put time and effort into writing a post, usually receive good monetary compensation for their work. Some of the blogs offer valuable, specialty information that is not readily available from any other source. Consider finding those blogs:

- Use the **Bing.com** search engine and sign up for their points program.

- Input phrases such as: Writer Guidelines, Freelance Blogging Jobs, Write for Us, Submission Guidelines and Get Paid to Write

- Use first two pages of results because old information usually starts with the third page

An independent search (free of advertising) such as this will bring lucrative sources of income for professional bloggers.

Goodies from Grants

When you need money, but do not know how you could possibly pay back a loan, consider a grant. Unlike a loan, there is no expectation of repayment for a grant award. It is only necessary to understand requirements of the funding source and follow their guidelines.

A grant writer is the best resource for finding the most compatible money sources. That writer knows how to identify appropriate funding sources for any project. You will choose from crowd-funding, non-profits, foundations or government agencies.

Possible Income Scenarios

Good grant writers are not cheap. However, a grant writer has the expertise to find the right source(s) and determine the amount of money necessary to move a project forward. A grant writer conducts an initial interview with onsite researchers, managers and key staff members who will provide oversight for a project. This gleans valuable information for the writing of a proposal.

The writer needs to prepare a budget, which accompanies the proposal to the funding source. It outlines key activities, costs that apply to those key activities and monies to pay the evaluators for their reports. Grant writers may also negotiate the final contracts with funding sources after a proposal reaches acceptance.

Some grant writers will stay on to administer the contract after the funding occurs. According to Salary.com, United States grant writers earn an average income of $56,000 annually. Statistics from the upper and lower 10% reveal that beginners in the field could earn an average of $27,000 annually and a seasoned professional might be able to pull in $99,000 or more.

The cost of grant making depends on the sponsor and breadth of the project they are funding. A grant could span a specific period or it might be continuous or renewable. Grant writers follow the money to a variety of sources including charitable entities, non-profits, federal or state governments, public or private foundations and registered philanthropists.

Online Education and Continuing Education

Continuing Education is a requirement to retain some positions, especially if you are a professional or technical worker. Writers are professionals who should take this seriously in order to keep up with benefits, technology and writing niches. It is important to stay one-step ahead of the rest of the crowd.

There are a number of courses, seminars and workshops for grant writers available through writer groups. Knowing this as well as the fact that a majority of writers are not well versed in grant writing, this is easy to rectify. An online course - or two - is enough to immerse you in the field of grant writing.

Learning to write grants could begin here:

American Grant Writers Association (Introductory Course = $249.00 USD)
http://www.agwa.us/agwa.us/training

Free Money and Small Grants (Micro-financing in the United States)
http://www.gofreegovernmentmoney.com/

The Grantsmanship Center (5-day training = $895)
http://www.tcgi.com/training/grantsmanship-training-program-5-day

Win Government Grants (Information and Guidance)
http://www.gofreegovernmentmoney.com/

Federal Grant Reform

Federal grant reform became reality as of December 2014. The Office of Management and Budget (OMB) jointly with the Council on Federal Assistance Reform (COFAR) made that public announcement. For anyone who is interested in downloading the specifics, a link with full explanation is available through The Grantsmanship Center (http://www.tcgi.com).

Government awarding agencies each are rolling out new regulations by the end of December 2014. A "super circular" about grant awards is available from each granting agency. The circular should indicate all the audit, administration and costs necessary for each agency.

Eight blogs appear on the government site and explain each part of this super circular. At the time of this printing, the requirements and project coverage are different for each funder you are considering. You can also submit an application to more than one funder at the same time.

Grants for Writers

Yes, even the writer may need a grant. This list of grants and funding sources focuses on the needs of most writers.

The most significant contribution of grant sources specific to writers and their needs comes from the author/writer C. Hope Clark. Her newsletter, Funds for Writers, has a grant list within each issue.

- C. Hope Clark (Funds for Writers) http://www.fundsforwriters.com/

- Catalog of Federal Domestic Assistance (grants/loans) http://www.cfda.gov/

- **Furthermore.org** (grant maker) http://furthermore.org

- **Grants.gov** (federal grants for individuals) http://www.grants.gov/web/grants/home.html

- **From the Heart Productions** (writer/film-maker grants) http://fromtheheartproductions.com/roy-w-dean-grants/

- National Endowment for the Arts (grant maker) http://arts.gov/grants

- NC Arts Council (grant maker) http://www.ncarts.org/grants

- PEN American Center - Writers' Emergency Fund (grant maker) http://staging.pen.org/writers-emergency-fund-eligibility-requirements

- **ProofPositive.com** (Canadian grants and grant writing) http://proofpositive.com/contests/canadian-writers-grants/

- **Society of Author's British Charitable Trust** (grant maker) http://www.societyofauthors.org/grants-and-prizes

- Stephen King's Haven Foundation (grant maker)
  http://www.thehavenfdn.org/

- **VoelkerFoundation.org** (grant maker) http://voelkerfdn.org/

- **Writing-World.com** (database of links to grant makers)
  http://writingworld.com/links/grants.shtml

Crowdfunding

Crowdfunding is another route offering immediate rewards. It is easier than applying and conducting proper follow-through with grant funding. It is not the same as asking for a loan with interest rates and term periods.

Consider the types of crowdfunding that are available: all-or-nothing funding, equity crowdfunding (learn this from Shark Tank) and percent funding.

Certain projects will reach a funding goal faster than the traditional grant or foundation funding. Explore the possibilities in this crowded field of crowdfunding sites through the Essential List of Crowd funding Websites (http://crowdfundingwebsites.net/) database to find your personal favorite.

Most people are familiar with certain crowd funding sites like www.kickstarter.com file://localhost/(http/::www.kickstarter.com) or the website www.ModestNeeds.org (http://www.modestneeds.org).

Crowd funding sites are multiplying like bunnies across planet Earth. Some sites encourage global participation. All sites require your marketing activities to promote the project for funding.

At this moment, these databases lead to many of the crowdfunding venues:

Early Shares - business
(http://earlyshares.com)

Funded.com - business
(http://www.funded.com/)

GoGetFunding.com - individual needs
(http://gogetfunding.com/)

GoFundMe.com - individual needs
(http://www.gofundme.com/)

IndieGoGo.com - business and individual needs
(http://www.indiegogo.com/)

Kickstarter.com - creative projects
(https://www.kickstarter.com/)

ModestNeeds.org - individual expenses
(http://www.modestneeds.org/index.asp)

RocketHub.com - personal projects
(http://www.rockethub.com/)

<u>Making Magazine Money</u>

Traditionalists seem to find it more pleasurable to write for hard copy print formats. New freelance writers who would like to write for these sources find it troubling to spend most of their time waiting rather than writing. The internet brings both of these groups together rather nicely.

With the advent of tablets and eReaders, many of the hard copy formats produce their information for electronic readers. Publishers recognize that it is much easier to toss an eReader into your pocket, handbag or backpack than to carry along an unwieldy newspaper or a stack of books. Writers need to be where the readers hang out.

Hard Copy Publishing

Hard copy magazine publishers realize that readers like online venues. Therefore, the publisher wanting to remain viable needs to be where the readers are trending. This means magazines should be publishing e-format information for electronic or internet reading.

Traditional hard copy writers are beginning to understand this shift to online writing. Currently, that is the path to a sustainable life income and every writer needs to follow the money trail. Below are listings that link to good income sources - either upon acceptance of your submission or upon publication.

Note that "upon acceptance" may pay less, but you get payment faster. "Upon publication" could keep you waiting for years, but you get much healthier payments for your work. Some entries have live links that take you to databases featuring groups of publishers looking for freelance writers. Most entries in these databases are gems that pay well. You will not find any residual income or bid-for-work sites here.

Magazines Accepting Freelance Writers

Abilities magazine looks for Canadian writers who will write articles of 500-2000 words for honoraria compensation in the range of $50-$325.
http://abilities.ca/writers-guidelines/

Adventure Cyclist accepts writers worldwide who will write articles for payment of $0.30-$0.45 per word. http://www.adventurecycling.org/adventure-cyclist/adventure-cyclist-submissions/writing-guidelines/

Alaska Airlines Magazine seeks writers from the United States for articles of 200-2500 words and payment ranging from $150-$700 per article. http://www.alaskaairlinesmagazine.com/contributor/guidelines/

Alive Now! accepts 400+ word submissions from United States writers for payment of $35. http://alivenow.upperroom.org/writers/

American Profile prefers United States writers to submit articles of 350-1000 words for payment negotiated in advance as well as a writer's profile. http://360.athlonmediagroup.com/

Bead & Button Magazine is open to North American writers who can submit feature articles of 1000-1200 words with a payment ranging from $75-$400. http://bnb.beadandbutton.com/about-us/submission-guidelines/

Beta Magazine is part of the Matador Network and seeks writers worldwide with a story to tell. They are new, edgy and do not pay travel expenses … yet. Payment is currently $0.50 per word when the article query gets an approval. http://matadornetwork.com/betamag/writers-guidelines/

Bird Talk Magazine works with writers worldwide and seeks articles of 800-2000 words with photos in exchange for compensation ranging from $100-$400. http://www.birdchannel.com/bird-magazines/bird-talk-2004-03-10-12850.aspx

CatholicDigest.com appears to accept writers worldwide to pen articles of 200-1500 words. Compensation ranges from $100-$500 per article. http://www.catholicdigest.com/writers_guidelines.html

Children's Writer seeks United States writers with articles of 750-2000 words and gives compensation of $200-$300. http://childrenswriter.com/guidelines.htm

Coastal Living Magazine works with United States writers and offers compensation of $1 per word. http://www.coastalliving.com/general/about-us

Dialogue Magazine seeks writers worldwide for articles of 200-1000 words at a pay range of $15-$35. Vision-impaired writers have priority. http://www.blindskills.com/submit.html

Dig Magazine seeks writers worldwide who are passionate about sharing history with children ages 9-14. They pay up to $200 p/article and $100 for images. https://www.cricketmag.com/26-Submission-Guidelines-for-DIG-magazine-for-children-ages-9-14

Dollars & Sense works with United States writers only for articles of 250-3000 words for undisclosed, negotiated compensation. http://www.dollarsandsense.org/write.html

DollarStretcher.com is a site for United States writers with both an online and offline presence. However, it only pays for articles for the print version. They offer $0.10 per word. http://stretcher.com/menu/writers.cfm

Family Handyman.com accepts submissions from readers in North America for payment of $100 if your article meets their guidelines for publication. https://www.familyhandyman.com/access/login?ReturnURL=/SubmitStory/Index

Family Tree Magazine is accepting short, niche articles from North American writers with pay relative to length and intensity of information. They pay on acceptance. http://www.familytreemagazine.com/article/writersguidelines

Green Prints Magazine seeks articles (less than 2000 words) from native English language writers for compensation of $150 per article. http://www.greenprints.com/content/12-writer-guidelines

Highlights for Children accepts United States writers for various department articles with each department administering their own payments for writers. https://www2.highlights.com/contributor-guidelines

History Magazine seeks feature-length articles that focus on the period from the Roman Empire to 1959 and pays eight cents per word and $7.00 USD per illustration. Read more in their writer guidelines. http://www.history-magazine.com/anotes.html

Hobby Farms Home accepts articles from United States writers with 500-2000 words for payment ranging from $50-$300. http://www.hobbyfarms.com/corporate/hfh-writer-guidelines.aspx

In the Know Traveler pays worldwide writers $10 for well-written articles and blog posts of 450 words. The writer retains all rights.
http://intheknowtraveler.com/about-us/submission-guidelines/

International Living Magazine accepts worldwide x-pat writers to write 500-600 words for payment of $75. http://internationalliving.com/about-il/write-for-il/

Italian America seeks United States writers who will write articles of 750-1000 words for payment of $100-$250. http://www.osia.org/ia-magazine/freelance-guidelines.php

Law and Order Magazine seeks United States writers who can write 1800-2400 words to inform readers and will make payment of $0.10 to $0.25 per word. http://www.hendonpub.com/submitting_articles/freelance_writers_guidelines

Little India Magazine looks for writers from around the world who are natives of India and who can provide 500-3500 word articles for a pay range of $50-$700 depending upon the article. http://www.littleindia.com/writers.html

Mortgage Banking Magazine seeks North American writers to provide 1000-2500 word articles for payment negotiated prior to submission. http://www.mortgagebankingmagazine.com/WritersGuidelines.htm

Oregon Coast Magazine seeks regional United States travel writers to submit articles for various departments with a range of 450-3000 words and payment ranging from $100-$650. http://www.oregoncoastmagazine.com/guidlin.php

Oregon Quarterly welcomes regional United States writers (familiar with Oregon and the University of Oregon) willing to write articles of 400-1000 words for compensation of $100-$350 per article. http://www.oregonquarterly.com/guidelines-for-contributors

Poets and Writers Magazine accepts submissions from worldwide writers for articles of 500-3000 words with compensation that varies per article and article length. http://www.pw.org/about-us/submission_guidelines

Pyragraph.com is a magazine for career-minded folk around the world. Writers must produce a minimum of 250 words to receive a pre-agreed payment. http://www.pyragraph.com/communitybloggers/community-blogger-guidelines/

Quilter's World seeks designer writers worldwide to contribute patterns, directions and tips with compensation negotiated before submission. http://www.quiltersworld.com/designer_guidelines.php

Reader's Digest welcomes writers worldwide to contribute "shorties" to certain departments for compensation up to $400. http://www.rd.com/magazine/submissions/

Ruralite accepts articles from United States writers with 100+ words for payment ranging from $50-$500. https://www.ruralite.org/learn-more/writers-guidelines/

Scrap is a trade journal that prints contributions from United States writers and pays $600-$1000 upon acceptancefile://localhost/. http/::www.writejobs.info:2011:05:freelance-writing-scrap-magazine-pays.html

Sierra is a magazine for environmental awareness and accepts United States writers who can submit articles of 100-5000 words for compensation ranging from $50-$1000 and/or $0.75 per word depending upon article length and depth. http://www.sierraclub.org/sierra

Subtropics will accept submissions from writers worldwide and compensates them with $500-$1000 while poets earn $100 per poem. http://subtropics.english.ufl.edu/submissions/

Take a Break Magazine does not specify writer location. This is a lifestyle magazine about love and life. Compensation is £2,000 or $3,000 for articles that meet their guidelines. http://www.takeabreak.co.uk/sell-us-your-story

Vermont Life works with United States writers willing to write standard articles for payment of $600 and feature articles for $800. http://vermontlife.com/guidelines-for-contributors/

Yankee Magazine accepts submissions from United States writers containing 600-1400 words and offers compensation of $25 per article. http://www.yankeemagazine.com/contact/guidelines

Writing for Dollars represents a group of publications that focus on saving money, living frugally and providing for an independent life. Writer guidelines - as of 2018 - are current for all publications in this list. The magazines they list have both an online AND offline presence.

It is possible that publications may abandon (or combine) their dual offerings to become electronic publications due to the popularity of portable eReaders. You can plan for a slow and steady transition. They need skilled writers to provide content for both types of reader - and the money trail is winding in that direction.

Writers who maintain a blog want to find ways to "make it pay" at least enough to cover the upkeep it requires. Forget the banners, links or visuals where you may have affiliate relationships. If you want to make your blog pay you as a writer, there is only one lucrative way to do it.

Crowd Appeal

Product reviews draw a crowd. That crowd will read the information on your blog and follow a link to the product location. Like most crowds, some are lookers and some are buyers. The buyers are the ones that could bring in your profit.

It is not necessary to have a blog dedicated to product reviews. You will have the same or better return if the products relate to the topic of your blog. Any product you decide to review should be an item you have tested, bought or used in some way.

Balanced Information

A personalized review draws a better crowd than a bland explanation of the fine functional qualities of your select product. Reviews should be balanced and present both the negative and positive points of the product. There are various paths you can travel as a writer using this process.

If your Consumer Search blog talks about the parts of speech or marketing your work with every posting, you are less likely to retain a following. However, for every five posts on your blog, one or two could review products.

Start with the Obvious

Writers who feature product reviews have a wide range of coverage selection. Start with the obvious. eReaders are everywhere with production of them in the hands of a number of companies.

Each eReader is a good subject for either a stand-alone review or the comparison review, which evaluate unique features. Writers are not "quill and parchment" people any more. Their choice of equipment is the laptop.

With so many laptops and tablets to choose from, a good review of the various types and available features would make some helpful postings.

Writers Are Readers

After all, writers are coming to the point where writing is only half of their working lives. Today, it is important that a writer knows a few "techie" tricks and the first of these is knowledge of the computing device they use that performs first time, every time.

Not only does a writer pay strict attention to their own works, they also read works by other writers. They are especially busy and curious folk who like to know what is out there for - or against - them. This is certainly the case of works by writers about writing, formatting or marketing writing of their own.

Some writers do reviews that influence other writers in some way. Do you want to receive compensation for writing about products? At Amazon.com you can earn real money for your efforts. Just scroll to the bottom of their home page to find out more about this opportunity.

Write Some Reviews

Certain writers have a reputation that precedes them by virtue of their seniority in the writing arena. New writers deserve no less and that is where the product review could become a huge stepping-stone for a writing career.

There are online sources that pay for product reviews. These are just a few of the sites that thrive on contributions from writers reviewing various products:

    Amazon.com http://www.amazon.com
    Consumer Search http://www.consumersearch.com
    Sponsored Reviews http://www.sponsoredreviews.com/bloggers.asp
    Writer Magazine http://www.writermagazine.com

Writers usually maintain a personal blog and can incorporate product reviews into the niche topic. In order to do this most effectively, they turn to a blogging host that provides the most professional presentation with the least technical platform that is possible. Most will head over to the highly promoted

WordPress blogging sites (wordpress.com and wordpress.org) without realizing the plethora of other sites available.

Free to Use - Mostly

WebSmarts, Weebly, Wix and Yola are all set up with available free templates and can accommodate a blog or a website with up to five pages of supporting and related material. Of course, you can also use blog platforms by Google, Yahoo or AOL.

Be aware that if you choose the free route, you might also give up some rights to your own material. Read terms and conditions carefully to ensure that the right to all posts and archives belong to you forever. Perhaps, you could find a host that features free templates and adapt a site to serve as your blog.

<u>Self Promotion</u>

Meanwhile, as much as you think otherwise, a writer should have a basic website. Use some of your "waiting" time to put a basic profile online. A short and professional autobiography, a few live links to articles you have written and/or a portion of your CV/resume should suffice.

The WYSIWYG Option

Good news for new writers: There are WYSIWYG formats available so you can get your material up and active. WYSIWYG means "What You See Is What You Get" and allows you to design and populate your site quickly without technical knowledge.

Now, writers with no graphic design or website design are able to start and maintain a site that they own. This is both cost-effective and convenient. With some skill over time, a non-technical person can be professional and present a good-looking experience to visitors.

Buyers Want to Know

If you wish to make a general statement about your rates or writing within a special niche, do so with ease. You can direct visitors to your blog or a guest post that you wrote.

Allena Tapia is a writer for http://www.about.com who did an informative column addressing the issue of freelance writing rates. It is one of the first questions posed by writers entering the world of freelancing. Most writers want to give visitors to a blog or website some idea of the cost of their services.

She shares the following information on this topic as a general guideline for new writers.

Freelance Writing Rates by Project
by Allena Tapia
http://www.about.com

Advertising/Copywriting
Mail Pieces (no graphics) $300 - $3000

Advertising/Copywriting
Sales Letter $150 - $2000

Articles
(news or significant research, web-based) $15 - $50

Articles (magazine) $150 - $5000+

Articles (content/keyword) $15 - $50
Articles (newspaper) $75 - $1000

Books (ghost-writing) $2 - $80 per page

Book Reviews $2 - $100

Book Summaries $250 to $500 p/book

Brochures $300 - $2500
(no graphic work)

Business Plans $500 - $5000

Editorial Management
(magazine/per issue) $500 - $5000

Grant Writing $200 - $5000+

Newsletters $200 - $1000

Press Release $200 - $500

Resume $200 - $500

Scripts $1000 - $20,000+

Of course, Allena Tapia's column shares more than this. This list shows a range of possibilities for most of the popular writing projects. You can pick your offerings from that list.

The items you choose should be items that you can immediately produce. As you acquire new skills, your list will expand and the prices may rise.

Are You for Real?

A professionally sharp image of the real YOU is more than an asset. It is a necessity. Your visitors may become clients and they want to be able to trust in a real, live person. For that reason, avatars are not appropriate in place of your picture.

Make sure you provide contact information, especially if you want potential clients to reach you. Pay for your web domain name (your own name is best), use free or low-cost hosting and you are good to go.

In the past, the white paper was an academic and/or technical foray not meant for the faint of heart. The truth is that white papers shrank since then in the same way that data became so much bigger. We are a world full of short attention span people who make cryptic comments on Facebook or Twitter in an electronic language.

Who Does This?

A writer needs to meet members of a target audiencs in their comfort zone without pushing the envelope too far. Busy people do not have time to do any in-depth reading. This applies from top-level managers to the pre-teen neighborhood kid.

When they reach for the computing device, they become scanners. If it means that your target audience is a group of scanners then it follows that you must come to the point with clarity - and fast. This planet does not have that many people who can do that effectively.

Professional writers can easily learn this technique if it is not part of them already.

Keep It on Track

Since the number of writers who work with white papers is rather lean, this is pioneer territory. There are a few specialists, who are willing to make their knowledge FREELY available to other writers. If you have never heard of people such as Jonathan Kantor, Perry Marshall or Michael Stelgman, it means you are out of the loop where white papers exist.

It should be clear for most content writers that people prefer to get their information from short articles. They need to be able to scan for important data and come away with only the highlights. Either hire a good editor to cut out 40% of the content and still keep 70% of its value or be ready to do this yourself.

Three Principles

You have three guiding principles that you can use to produce a big impact with "scan" readers who have short attention spans. These are simple to follow and easy to understand.

Plan your white paper length: A short white paper should be 2 - 5 pages in order to provide enough information without crushing the short attention span reader. If the topic is technical in nature, the reader will likely be in research or technology and these areas do not lend themselves to a short white paper. Short white papers of less than six pages tend to focus on problem- solving consumer issues and are not useful in thoroughly educating the technological business professional.

Enhance the short white paper with attention-grabbing techniques. could use a sidebar, shaded text boxes, short bullet lists or a combination of these. This practice gives the reader short, clear messages much like the 140-character Twitter message.

Two summaries should be included: an executive summary and a concluding summary. This inclusion does not alienate your short attention span readers, but it will assist the business reader with key "bottom line" information. Consider including charts or graphs in the sidebar with an explanation below the image.

The Guru Experts

As I mentioned at the start of this section, some specialists - ala gurus - are willing to share wisdom and insights with writers wishing to enter this niche. They include:

1) **American Writers & Artists, Inc** is publisher of Six Steps to Writing a Successful White Paper by John Wood. He explains that writers who are just starting out should be able to get a minimum of $2500 for a white paper. Each paper takes at least 30-50 hours from start to finish.
http://www.awaionline.com/

2) Graham, Gordon. **That White Paper Guy** is the author/writer of White Papers for Dummies. He offers FREE information and advice as well as a monthly newsletter with tips to use when writing a white paper.
http://www.awaionline.com/bio/gordon-graham/

3) Kantor, Jonathan. **Short Attention Marketing** is the subject of his blog, The White Paper Pundit. He is founder of The Appum Group, also known as The White Paper Company.

4) Marshall, Perry. His blog tells you how to write a white paper, which does not need to be a tedious chore. As a matter-of-fact, this could be straightforward, pleasant and amazingly enjoyable. Perry also offers a FREE email course: **Attract More Customers with White Papers.**
http://www.entrepreneur.com/author/perry-marshall

5) Stelzner, Michael. **Writing White Papers** is the name of his blog, book and FREE course, which is available for visitors to that blog. It is in five parts and each appears on the front page of his blog.
http://www.writingwhitepapers.com/book/index.htm

Be wise as you use the information in this report. It is best that you select more than one type of writing for your own security.

What would happen if client requests dry up for a short time on your chosen site or writing site - or a writing site comes under new management? The perceptive writer picks a number of sources (perhaps one from each section of this book) to alternate between them for gigs.

As more writer guidelines become available online or others disappear, the changes will find their way into this directory. The writer guidelines for sources already here show live URL links in almost all cases.

Get Your Free Copy

Writers purchasing this directory are eligible for a free copy when an update becomes available.

Send a copy of your purchase invoice as an email attachment (showing the best email address that you check most often) to write2earn@aol.com. I will add you to my update list.

Everything changes so fast in today's world: new writing sites come online and old standby sites change their guidelines or disappear. Some sites might stop accepting writer applications because the writer pool is saturated. (Somewhere, this might be an "excuse" rejection, but not in the true sense of the word.)

Paying Market Databases

Following is a list of databases that contain ever-changing entries. Some of the entries are already part of this directory and others are brand new. Since I have not checked all entries in the databases yet, please let me know if you use a database that does not appear here. I would like to visit the site and include it - if it fits the criteria for inclusion.

- BeaconReader.com (international) http://www.beaconreader.com/

• Catalog of Federal Domestic Assistance (US grants/loans)
https://www.cfda.gov/?s=generalinfo&mode=list&tab=list

• FreelanceWriting.com (worldwide)
http://www.freelancewriting.com/guidelines/pages/index.php

• Grants.gov (US) http://www.grants.gov/web/grants/search-grants.html

• GrantsforWriters (UK) http://www.societyofauthors.org/grants-writers-need

• GrantSpace.org (US) http://grantspace.org/

• GrantWriters.net (US) http://grantwriters.net/

• JournalismGrants.org (international) http://journalismgrants.org/

• LegitimateOnlineJobs.com (international)
http://www.legitimateonlinejobs.com/?hop=nickaffi

• NextJobAtHome.net (US) http://www.typingwritingjobs.com/

• FreelanceWritersNeeded.com http://www.freelancewritersneeded.com/

• OpenSocietyFoundations.org (international)
https://www.opensocietyfoundations.org/grants

• ProspectSolution (UK) http://www.prospectsolution.com/

• PulitzerCenter.org http://pulitzercenter.org/grants

• Small Business Grants for Women (US)
http://www.smallbusinessgrants.biz/

• StayOnSearch.com (worldwide) http://www.stayonsearch.com/write-for-us
• SunOasis.com (worldwide) http://www.sunoasis.com/

• TheFoundationCenter.org (worldwide)
http://gtionline.foundationcenter.org/?_ga=1.37037344.1088785417.1417920275

- Typing, Writing and Blogging Jobs (worldwide)
http://www.typingwritingjobs.com/

- WorkersOnBoard.com (worldwide) http://www.workersonboard.com/

- WorldwideFreelance.com (worldwide)
http://www.worldwidefreelance.com/markets/

- WritersWrite.net (worldwide)
http://www.writerswrite.com/writersguidelines/

Move on with the knowledge that there are more than 200 sources for international working writers including many grant-funding sources in this directory. In addition to those numbers, the list of databases here leads to a multiple amount of additional writing sources for you.

My last word would be a quote from a poet that I feel every author and writer should follow:

It Couldn't Be Done
Edgar Albert Guest
(http://www.poetryfoundation.org/bio/edgar-albert-guest)

Somebody said that it couldn't be done
But he with a chuckle replied
That "maybe it couldn't," but he would be one
Who wouldn't say so till he'd tried.

So he buckled right in with the trace of a grin
On his face. If he worried he hid it.
He started to sing as he tackled the thing
That couldn't be done, and he did it!

Somebody scoffed: "Oh, you'll never do that;
At least no one ever has done it;"
But he took off his coat and he took off his hat
And the first thing we knew he'd begun it.

With a lift of his chin and a bit of a grin,
Without any doubting or quiddit,

He started to sing as he tackled the thing
That couldn't be done, and he did it.

There are thousands to tell you it cannot be done,
There are thousands to prophesy failure,
There are thousands to point out to you one by one,
The dangers that wait to assail you.

But just buckle in with a bit of a grin,
Just take off your coat and go to it;
Just start in to sing as you tackle the thing
That "cannot be done," and you'll do it.

Best wishes for a wonderful and fulfilling adventure with your writing!
Follow your muse … wherever it may lead you.

###

9 781721 973767